A DANCE IN THE STREET

For Roland John
with respect, and thanks,
and very best wishes —
Jared Carter

by Jared Carter

collections

A Dance in the Street
Cross this Bridge at a Walk
Les Barricades Mystérieuses
After the Rain
Work, for the Night Is Coming

chapbooks

Blues Project
Situation Normal
The Shriving
Millennial Harbinger
Pincushion's Strawberry
Fugue State
Early Warning

e-books

Time Capsule
Reading the Tarot

A Dance in the Street

poems

Jared Carter

WIND PUBLICATIONS
NICHOLASVILLE, KENTUCKY

A Dance in the Street. Copyright © 2012 by Jared Carter. Printed in the United States of America. All rights reserved. No part of this book may be reproduced in any manner except for brief quotations embodied in critical articles or reviews. For information, address Wind Publications, 600 Overbrook Drive, Nicholasville KY 40356

International Standard Book Number 978-1-936138-27-2
Library of Congress Control Number 2011925535

First edition

Front-cover photo: "Day," by *New York Times* photographer Edward Hausner. Reproduced by permission of Redux Pictures. Further information in "Acknowledgments."

Epigraph: from *Life with Picasso* by Françoise Gilot and Carleton Lake. Copyright © 1989 by Vintage/Anchor Books and reproduced by permission.

for Selene and Isaiah

What is the price of Experience? do men buy it for a song?
Or wisdom for a dance in the street?
— William Blake

Contents

One	Prophet Township	3
	Roadside Crosses	6
	Natural Gas Boom	7
	Miss Hester	10
	Difficult	11
	Summit	15
Two	Fire Burning in a 55-Gallon Drum	19
	East Washington Street Plasma Center	20
	In the Warehouse District	21
	Triage	22
	In the Military Park	25
	The Pool at Noon	26
	Plastic Sack	29
Three	Hidden Door	33
	Wind Egg	34
	Soul Sleeping	36
	Stars in Daylight	38
	Truth to Tell	42
	Nether Moon	44
	What Is Dream?	46
Four	Sphinx	49
	Colossi of Memnon	50
	Senmurv	53
	Kloster Wienhausen	56
	Menuki	58
	War	60
	At the Art Institute	61

Five	Slab Wood	67
	Up in Michigan	70
	Maysville, Simon Kenton Bridge, Dusk	73
Six	Encounter	81
	Blank Paper	83
	Under the Snowball Bush	86
	Mourning Dove Ascending	88
	Cicadas in the Rain	89
	Snow	90

Acknowledgments	95
About the Author	99

There was Daumier, too, in the stones themselves. Many of the stones at Mourlot's had been in use since well back in the nineteenth century. After each impression the stone is rubbed down to remove the drawing. But since lithographic stone is limestone, soft and porous, it absorbs a bit of the ink and an impression of the drawing penetrates beneath the surface. Portions of an old drawing occasionally seep back up to the surface again after a stone has been rubbed down. Lithographers call that the stone's "memory" and occasionally we would see one of the stones "recalling" a passage from Daumier.

— Françoise Gilot,
Life with Picasso

A Dance in the Street

One

Prophet Township

Only that it was a place where snow
and ice could seal off whole sections
for half the winter, where the ground —
even when you dug down to it — could not
be budged.
         If you had someone to bury,
you waited for spring thaw. Children
died from diphtheria and scarlet fever,
old-timers came down with pneumonia,
horses reared up suddenly in the barn.

The coffin would be kept in the parlor
for three days and nights. The watchers
took turns. After the funeral, neighbors
helped carry the box up to the attic
or set it out in one of the back rooms
so it would stay cold but not freeze.
Before the men tacked down the lid,
they filled it up the rest of the way
with rock salt. This was a custom
learned from their grandparents —
how to make it through till spring,
how to handle hardship on their own.
But there were times when no one lasted,
fierce winters when the wood gave out,
when there was nothing left to eat,
no hay to pitch out for the stock,
no way to break down through the ice
on the horse trough, or get the pump
working again.

                    With no heat, no money
for seed, they knew they had no choice
but to pack up and leave — head back
to town, try to get a stake together,
go somewhere else. They brought along
what they could carry. Everything else
was left behind: piles of old clothes,
root cellar full of empty Mason jars,
strings of peppers tied to the rafters.

This is a long migration, a traveling
back and forth, over many harsh years.
Even now, people move off the land —
realize they're not going to make it,
understand there's no point in trying.
The old farmhouses are stripped clean,
emptied out, made ready for lightning
or for a final warming fire built
in the middle of the parlor floor
by some transient, some jobless family
camped for the night.
                    Grass grows
knee-high around the pump, the catalpa
holds up its brown and purple flowers.
Wind, searching along the kitchen shelf,
knocks a last jelly glass to the floor.
Soot bleeds from the hole in the wall
where the flue once went in.
                    By December
if no fire breaks out, cold weather
clamps down. The freeze and thaw
eats at the plaster — spitting out nails,

breathing in dust, over and over —
gnawing it to the marrow.
                      Now and then
when I drive past one of these places
set back up the lane — doors unhinged,
windows broken out, lilacs choked up,
willow drooping in the side yard —
I'm never in much of a hurry to stop,
poke around.
                Sometimes I sit there
in the driveway for a few minutes,
thinking about it, knowing that if I
step up to the front porch, or find
my way through the weeds to the pump,
there will be a slight breath of wind
just ahead of me, something rustling
through the timothy grass.
                     It will pause,
stopping each time I do, waiting
until everything gets quiet again.
I can't catch up with it, or come
face to face with whatever it is.
I can sense only that it's pleased —
by the way it turns, every so often,
to make sure I'm still coming.

Roadside Crosses

This is a state where nothing marks the spot
officially. They crop up now and then
out on the freeway, or in rustic plots
sometimes, near S-curves in the country, when
the corn's knee-high. A cross, or even two
or three, made out of poles or boards, white-
washed or painted. They seem to have a view
of nothing at all, only the blurred lights
of oncoming cars, and the eighteen-wheelers
roaring by. Memory has a harsh sting —
blown back like the fine grit that settles
while you walk here now, no special healer,
merely a friend or brother, stopped to bring
a can of flowers, to place among the nettles.

Natural Gas Boom

"It was a kind of rhythm," she said, stirring
ever so slightly in the porch swing, until
it creaked to a stop. I could not quite see her —
interval of first firefly, evening star.

"I was ten years old when they discovered it.
Towns with five hundred people shot up
to five thousand. They thought the millennium
had come, that the gas would last forever.

"They walked with a swagger — proud of the way
they wasted it. They let the streetlamps burn
night and day. Too much trouble to hire a man
to go around and put them out each morning."

She was silent for a moment. It was long ago.
"My stepmother had my father sign up to pay
for workmen to run a pipe out to our side yard,
to give light. A dollar a month. It was called

a flambeau. It was never supposed to go out.
For an innocent farm girl, it was like the pillar
of smoke by day and fire by night that led Moses
and the children of Israel to the promised land."

She had spoken of that house before. How once,
a photographer came, and posed father, stepmother,
her own brother, Glenn, her two stepbrothers
and her stepsister, with the house behind them.

She recalled her father wore a Democratic badge;
it must have been at about the time of Cleveland's
second inaugural. And the boys, how they fancied
long mustaches, waxed and curled, like those

of villains they saw in plays at the opera house.
Her stepmother wound her hands in her best apron.
My grandmother wore a new straw hat and gloves.
I never saw the photo, it was lost before I was born.

Sometimes she talked about it — how expectant
they all looked, standing there. The gas would
continue to flow for ten more years, forming
a ring of factories and foundries — a vast globe

of speculation hovering over the countryside,
casting no shadow. "I remember," she went on,
"how cold it was, that last morning, when the gas
finally gave out. Our flambeau had shut down.

We looked across the fields, toward town,
and everything was dark. The boom was over.
We heard people calling out, all that way —
they were ruined. They had lost everything."

Another silence. An evening chill had come on.
I sensed, for the first time, that the photographer
had made sure the house screened the flambeau
in the side yard — that what she remembered,

what she noticed, even in the way they posed,
back when they thought it would last forever —
how her three brothers seemed so cocky,
how she had clung to her stepsister's arm —

all of that was backlit by an elusive glow,
as though, standing behind them, invisible
in that earthly garden, some presence, terrible
and unforgiving, was about to lift its sword.

She had never been one for quoting scripture,
but she knew the stories. "Moses followed after
the pillar of fire," she said. "But in the end,
he was not allowed to enter the promised land."

It was late. She adjusted the frayed afghan
about her shoulders. The calls of katydids
and tree frogs had grown louder. She tapped
my hand. "It's time for us to go inside."

Miss Hester

"Are we entirely ready, then?" she asked,
and I knew by the threads of smoke drifting
through the light, through the empty beam —
I knew she could not form different faces
on the screen, but that no one else in town
could sit there and make music, or understand
what might follow. "I thought perhaps Schumann,"
she whispered, reaching to touch the keys.
The crowd was hushed. At the back of the hall
the projector's reels settled into a rhythm
and the first scene came into view. The film?
Something about being young, and leaving home,
going off to the city. She closed her eyes
and began to play, in the dark, and we looked up.

Difficult

He could not, in that moment, remember
where in the Book this had happened
before, whether among plagues of frogs
and mice, or brimstone raining down
on the heads of the unrighteous —
                              instead
could summon only the quavering calls
of mourning doves, out in the orchard,
where on days like this, the sweet mire
of fallen, neglected apples gave off
a scent that seemed interchangeable
with the murmur of bees —
                         but it had been
years since he could hear honeybees,
or cicadas, or distant thunder. Years
during which he had lived by himself
on the old place. Years since that day
they had carried her to the family plot,
at the far end of the eighty-acre field,
amid the pines and cedars. All that
more than a dozen years ago.
                         "Difficult,"
she had whispered, at the end,
"they said you were a difficult man."
She smiled, as though she understood
it had been otherwise. That smile
had stayed with him. But he was left
to wonder, three days later, standing
with the others, out in the grove,
if she were not sad to be leaving.

And so he had gone, once a year,
carrying a cone of newspaper filled
with the blue phlox she had tended,
to place against the stone. Had gone
to stand, with bowed head.
                              A difficult man.
A hard man, some said, to have wrestled
with that played-out farm all those years,
and never once considered taking her
and going elsewhere. Because his people
had been there from the beginning,
and were waiting, out in that grove.
Difficult. And a stiffness in his heart
that he could not explain. And now,
his hearing, his vision. On this visit,
he did not see, failed to notice, the clouds
to the south, their peculiar color. Ignored,
as he walked along, the wind picking up,
then dying, and the air suddenly chill.
Up ahead was the grove, its stones
tilted and dim, beneath the old trees.
He was far from the last barn or shed,
out in a vast empty field gone fallow.

Hail, when it first falls, bounces up
from hard surfaces, but there was nothing
except deep grass along that path. At first
it seemed someone was following him,
then the quick, sharp stings on his neck
and hands —
                it was all around him now,
smacking down, hammering hard,
the strange bluish stones becoming
bigger than any he had ever seen

before. Cold fists battered his face
and forearms, the bunch of phlox
flew from his grasp. The blossoms
scattered across the trail, beaten
and broken, the piece of newspaper
punched full of holes.

                       And nowhere
to turn. He was entirely without shelter.
It was half a mile to the grove, a mile
back to the first shed, and at his age
he could not run, could not make it,
could only drop to his knees, try
to roll into a ball, while the stones
kept banging away, pounding him
not in any sequence, but in bursts,
as though he were being kicked
again and again by some creature
with iron-shod hooves.

                           He lay there
twitching, hugging the ground, half
remembering plagues of hailstones,
blasphemers being punished, Saul
holding Stephen's coat, even Jesus
stepping in to admonish those
who had brought the woman taken
in adultery —

                but now it all seemed
far away, translucent pages fluttering
in the wind. Random stones bounced
against his shoulders, his skull,
final gestures that no longer seemed
difficult to grasp.

                     He began
to let go, like a ball of twine

that for years has been hidden
in some dry, sheltered place
and now has been brought out
into the wind, the blowing rain,
and is beginning to unwind,
to come apart. All around him,
gathered in icy drifts, the stones,
with their blue, crystalline hearts,
began to melt and disappear.

Summit

Small towns. A few houses and a general store.
The map might show only one road going through,
but if you keep driving around long enough,
you begin to understand how they're connected.
There are back roads running in all directions.
You just have to get out and look for them.

People living out there have known each other
for a long time. They still have family reunions
in late August, on plank tables under the trees.
Places with names like Hadley, and Springtown,
and Coatesville. Most of them manage to keep
a grain elevator going, maybe a post office.

I'm a real-estate appraiser. These days
I spend a lot of time out looking at farms.
I've got a bunch of good maps in my car;
old ones, too. You don't want to come back
to town and admit you couldn't even find
the place you were looking for. Or got lost.

One day last September I was driving along
a gravel road between Clayton and Hadley, using
an old county map. Up ahead was a little town
called Summit, that had been a flag stop once,
on a spur slanting off from the main line
to Terre Haute. That spur's been gone for years.

Summit was gone, too. But I found it, after
a while, figured out exactly where it had been,
right at the top of a long rise you could see

stretching for miles across the countryside.
Nothing out there now but lots of beans and corn,
blue sky and clouds. Not even fence rows anymore.

You could almost imagine the train heading west,
up that long grade, pouring on the coal, making
for high ground. When it finally pulled in,
and the telegraph man came out for the mail,
there would be a couple of little kids sitting
on the baggage wagon, waving to the engineer.

I walked up to the only place it could have been.
Right there, at the crest of the hill. Somebody
had kept it mowed. There was a strong wind blowing.
I searched around in the grass for a long time,
but I couldn't find anything. Not a trace.
Only the land itself, and the way it still rose up.

Two

Fire Burning in a 55-Gallon Drum

Next time you'll notice them on your way to work
or when you drive by that place near the river
where the stockyards used to stand, where everything

is gone now. They'll be leaning over the edge
of the barrel, getting it started — they'll step back
suddenly, and hold out their hands, as though

something fearful had appeared at its center.
Others will be coming over by then, pulling up
handfuls of weeds, bringing sticks and bits of paper,

laying them in gently, offering them to something
still hidden deep down inside the drum.
They will all form a circle, their hands almost

touching, sparks rising through their fingers,
their faces bright, their bodies darkened by smoke,
by flakes of ash swirling around them in the wind.

East Washington Street Plasma Center

It pays thirty dollars a visit. The line starts at six.
People who spend all day, searching for aluminum cans,
park their supermarket carts up and down the sidewalk.

When they turn on the lights he can see the front desk.
The attendants have papers on him. Every five days
they let him into the white room. He has done this

so many times he could lie there and stick the needle
in his own arm. The rest is easy. They drain a pint
of something out of him, but he does not believe

it is really blood, because they always put back
as much as they take out. They have told him
about plasma, shown him the centrifuge whirling,

even pointed out the place on the map where it goes —
somewhere in southern California. They do not realize
he controls things with his mind. Part of him stays

in California, inside other people, having a good time,
going to the track every day, winning, sending money home
to pay for more plasma. The other part is invisible,

it gets loose, there are people out looking for it,
trying to find it, but in five days it comes back,
all that way, and he is ready to go inside again.

In the Warehouse District

Once a man I know who deals in pianos and who takes anything
as a trade-in took me to a bricked-up building on a side street

on a day approaching 100 degrees, and with a coat-hanger key
let me inside a shuttered room filled with hundreds of pianos

so crowded together there was no space to walk between them.
All uprights, all damaged — cases nicked and scarred, keys missing —

all worthless and beyond repair. Four cast-iron pillars
stamped with ivy reached up to the corners of a skylight

boarded over with plywood. The lids of the pianos were thick
with soot and chunks of fallen plaster. All I could do was climb up

and walk around on top of them. The dealer stayed in the alley
and smoked a cigarette while I stepped from one dusty frame

to another, up higher than I should have been, going nowhere
in particular, occasionally hearing, beneath my feet, an echo,

a hollow stirring, as though some mechanism, some tension
still surviving, had registered my passing. Now and then I stopped

to kneel, to lean all the way over to an opened keyboard,
halfway expecting to see my own reflection there. Finally

reached down among the missing keys and touched a middle C —
listened to that single note ringing through the darkened room.

Triage

One

Nor does that interval return to me intact, and seldom
in the right sequence. After smoke, sometimes, if things
stay clear long enough — or a few drinks — I am driving

through a part of the country I have never seen before —
level farmland, western Illinois — on my way to a town
I know nothing about. I pull over and pick up a hitchhiker

who is cold and shivering, who says he's out of work,
he's been sick for a while, now he's going back to Templin,
where he still has people who remember him, who will take him in,

and where he hopes to find his father, and talk with him,
even though his father has been dead for fifteen years —
this said as though he had noticed a sign at the road's edge.

We drive along for a few miles. He wants to know if he can smoke.
He carries nothing with him, only the pack rolled in his sleeve.
He smokes, and looks out, and after a while goes on talking.

"My father is not really dead," he explains, "sometimes
he comes and stands where we can see him, across the river,
or maybe outside a restaurant. We look through the glass

and see him watching us." I glance across the flat land
we are driving through. "Do you speak to him?" I ask.
It is spring, the earth is dark and scored with furrows.

"It doesn't do any good," he replies. "He won't answer.
And if we try to get close, he goes away. Disappears."
He lights another cigarette and continues to talk,

reminiscing about earlier encounters. He remembers
being taken to the funeral when he was a little boy,
seeing them lower the coffin with his father's body inside —

but when he looked across the cemetery, he saw his father
standing near the gate, watching it all. "Why would he want
to do something like that?" I ask. "For the insurance money?

Why won't he see you now? Why has he done such a thing?"
"I don't know," the hitchhiker says, "that's why I'm going back.
I want to find him again. See if he will come any closer."

We are driving through Templin now. It is like everywhere else
I have never been before — same used-car dealers, same churches
and hamburger stands, same laundromat on the courthouse square.

Two

Years later in the place where I live — a burnt-out street
in a large inner city, with empty lots and frame houses covered
with aluminum siding and added-on porches made of glass blocks —

one of the young people who has grown up here explains to me
that the old ones have not really left, that they have not died,
that when it was time, they refused to go to nursing homes,

they have stayed here and found places for themselves
in the abandoned houses — buildings with boarded-up windows
and holes in the roof, paradise trees growing in the yard.

"They come back, they find shelter — maybe it was this house
they lived in for most of their lives, raised a family,
been somebody, paid taxes, once or twice had their names

in the paper, and now it's all over for them, everybody thinks
they are dead or in a home somewhere, but there is no money
for that, so they go on living in the shadow of their old life,

they only come out after dark. No one will look at them."
I ask "How do you know this?" but he turns away from me.
He has seen them, it is too painful for him to go on.

Three

Now it is night-time and you are the one who is driving alone
through darkened streets. Your car breaks down, rolls to a stop.
You get out. Somewhere up ahead there is a building on fire.

A man stumbles along the sidewalk — people may be chasing him,
you can hear their voices — sirens flare in the distance,
amber lights flicker — you cannot tell if he struggles to reach

your car or to escape from something else, but he is hurt,
he staggers toward you through the shadows. Spotlights
pick him out now — he is so close you can see into his eyes.

In the Military Park

At dawn, near the parade ground,
in the shadow of the obelisk,
where the fountains have not yet
been turned on, you can look out

and see the youthful instructor,
sometimes a man, usually a woman,
following five paces behind the one
who is blind, who is being taught

how to walk with a long, thin cane
that is swept from side to side
across the empty paths. They come
early, there is never anyone else

in the park at this hour. Immediately
after you drive by, you are not sure
you really understood what you saw.
It seems mixed up with something else,

some old, half-remembered story
that comes to you now, at the stoplight —
how she yearned to reach out and take
his hand, how he kept pressing ahead,

beyond the shadows, into the sunlight,
while she fell farther behind, and in
another moment, he will turn, and
there will be nothing, nothing at all.

The Pool at Noon

She is the secretary. She wears a bathing cap
of white rubber, to enclose her brittle hair,
and an elasticized suit of shirred green fabric.
She does not dive into the water, but descends,
backwards, down the shaky tubular ladder,
into the shallows, where the water is calm
and strangely luminous, and smells always
of chlorine —
            the echoes, among high girders
and skylights long ago painted over, of water
lapping in the scum-gutter, of dishes clinking,
far away, in the kitchen —
                   and everywhere,
across the glazed bottom and sides of the pool,
the shifting reflections and bands of soft light
in endless permutations —
                  she settles down
amid the ripples, spreads her arms, launches
herself, with her head back, into the stillness,
and begins her slow, symmetric sweeping.

We are in the YMCA of an ancient city
of abandoned mills and red-brick factories
that stretch along the river. This is the pool
built years ago, for the youth of the town,
when there was still some money. These days
the walls are pocked with broken tiles, the pipes
conveying the water are discolored with rust,
but still the elementary children of the town

are bussed here, and taught how to swim
by teen-aged instructors not much older
than themselves.
                      The children are brown
and black and pale white, they are separated
by gender, they swim naked, according to
an old custom, in this high-ceilinged pool
that booms with their squeals, their voices —
although now it is noon, they are dressed
and made to line up. Toting their backpacks,
herded outside, they form circles on the lawn,
and eat their lunch from plastic containers.

Here, in the pool's silence, and the constant
flickering of reflections, is the secretary,
who weekdays at this hour will backstroke
across the still water —
                          at the other end,
the deep end, is the pool maintenance man,
retired and in his seventies, with flaccid skin
and patches of grizzled hair on his arms
and legs and chest, who receives no pay,
and volunteers his services —
                          in order that
day after day, in his faded, baggy trunks
and his plastic nose-clip, he can climb up
and walk to the end of the 3-meter board,
and stand for a moment, and then step off
into the sheen of ever-shifting reflections
lining the pool's floor —
                          he becomes the shaft
of a needle slipped into impermanence,
he is that which almost touches something

balancing in the depths —
                        he bobs up again,
returns once more to the world of gaskets
and broken tiles and murmuring children.
Re-emerging, he floats improbably, since
he lacks bulk, and is nothing more than
a scarecrow, with white hair rayed out
around his head — but he has learned
how to hang motionless, arms extended,
only his face showing —
                        thus the rituals
of these two, who are old acquaintances,
but who do not speak — him suspended,
she progressing slowly across the shallows
with her eyes closed —
                        one moving, the other
drifting, and all around them the silence,
the placid water, the pale tremors of light
endlessly searching and shimmering.

Plastic Sack

Lifted by a warm current, ballooned
for a moment out of the slow swirl
of dust and paper cups blowing along
the alley, this diaphanous plastic bag —

product of modern technology, made
by the billions, the recyclable kind
you get at the checkout, when the clerk
asks you the inevitable question.

Upside down now, strangely inflated,
almost responsive, balanced among gusts
of wind, making no sound, its handles —
dangling loops — somehow reminding me

of snapshots of my father, on the porch,
that first autumn after the war ended,
wearing that slight, mostly forgotten
article of clothing, the undershirt.

But this is no revenant, no survivor
of those days. There are no features
on this face, nothing but a blankness
reflecting the light of the streetlamp

on the corner. It is only a plastic sack,
having come to the end of its journey,
almost aware that something is missing,
managing to rise up for one last look.

Three

Hidden Door

The old stories do not end the way you were told.
Hansel and Gretel do not escape from the witch's house;
they decide to stay. Ali Baba does not emerge from the cave
but enters a subterranean chamber that goes on for miles.

At every juncture there is always a hidden door.
When the characters step through, they enter a realm
having little resemblance to the world the rest of us know.
The old stories are never about what happens next,

but about the glass vial on the table. After days of heat,
you hear three sharp raps, and look out and see
winter hurrying through the forest — not rain or snow,
but a wind stripping the leaves and stiffening the grass.

Wind Egg

Once a wind egg called out to a young girl who went each morning
to collect eggs for her grandmother — "O child, do not take me,
let the hen my mother set for ten more days, I long to walk about
in the world, even now I can see the horse grazing in the meadow."

"How can this be?" the girl wondered. "Neither white egg nor brown
ever speaks to me. They have nothing to say, in their thin shells,
even when we hold them up to the candle's glow. But this one
has a blue eye, and wears no coat. I had better ask grandmother."

The old woman had peered into hens' eggs for so many years
she could see into the heart of things. When the child told her
of the talking egg, she was not deceived. "It is the wind,"
she declared, "trying to make mischief among honest folk."

"Never could we leave the brood mares alone in the pasture
when the wind blew up from the river. Crossing the barnyard
in winter, I too have felt it, reaching in. An egg without
a shell is an abomination. Cast it out for the hogs to eat!"

That night the girl dreamt of an empty nest, and a blue eye
singing to itself. She reached out to take it in her hand
but it was like holding water. She threw it against the wall
and it slid down and became whole again, balanced in her palm.

"No," she said to herself next morning, and she opened the pocket
of her apron and slipped in the strange egg. The black hen cackled,
and the rooster crowed. "Alas, I can see nothing!" the egg called,
but the girl's thighs kept it warm, and in nine days it quickened.

Lying alone in her room, she awoke to the glint of a new moon shining through the window, and there was no membrane, no shell, no barrier to what she could become. Next morning, the old woman looked away from the tremor of light into which she was gazing.

"Go," she said, "for nothing can keep you here now. That is the way of the wind — it is always blowing, always wanting to be elsewhere." She turned back to her candle. "I long to be out in the world," the young woman said. "The horse waits for me in the meadow."

The horse galloped toward her through the tall grass, and the wind leapt from her apron, into its sleek body, its churning hooves. The horse shuddered, and knelt down, and she mounted up. "Let us ride," said a clear voice that was all around her now.

Soul Sleeping

> *Doctors, medical staff, and family members should talk to comatose patients. . . . Brain-function tests indicate that some patients, though unable to respond, both hear and understand. And when cared for in silence, they may believe they are already dead.*
> — Archives of Neurology

Someone speaks. Perhaps you dreamed it even
while falling asleep — that time which is also
a place, when you drift off, and see, before
your eyes, nothing at all. It becomes, after
a while, more difficult to know, yet ever
more familiar, and coming closer, always.

The blind say that sounds have shadows: always
a different kind of light beckoning, even
summoning — not only toward silence, whatever
that might grow to be, as it spreads — but also
into safety. Something that remains after
the darkness is swept away, the part before.

To remember what that was like, before
it began, before answering became always
what happened next, think of a time after
the journey, when each sound or murmur, even
a voice crying in the night, could also
be your own, reflecting back on whatever

rises, from nowhere, to greet you. However
intangible, something was there before,
waiting. Recognizing it is all so

easy, but answering is hard. It always
seems to fade, in widening circles. Even
when it returns, you cannot speak, after

noticing such silence. Animals, after
they gaze in our eyes — creatures who never
say anything — still understand, even
when we ourselves no longer care. Before
we were old enough to reason, we always
believed in magic — a cat who would also

whisper, only to us, its secrets. Also
forgotten now, that long-ago time, after
you put on your pajamas. Someone always
read you a bedtime story. There was never
any regret that each tale ended before
it was over. Your breath came calm and even.

All so many go on dreaming. If no one ever
inquires after us, then what happened before
is always. What happens next — nothing, even.

Stars in Daylight

> *Our oldest reminiscences are the most alive and lasting.
> But they begin right at that point where the child has
> acquired sufficient language, they begin with those first
> ideas that we fused to signs and could fix in words. Like
> my own earliest memory, of some musk pears I saw and
> heard named in the same moment.*
> — Leopardi, *Zibaldone Di Pensieri,* May 28, 1821,
> translated by W. S. Di Piero

Hidden somewhere in memory — earliest, oldest trace
of objects gradually swimming into consciousness —
dust motes drifting in a shaft of sunlight, or the shock
of coldness in water — of being in some strange house
and handed a clear glass to drink from —
                                          while being
helped by an older person, the two of them holding
the glass, agreeing not to drop it while the child tilts it,
clinking his teeth against the rim, encountering the cold —
and in that same instant glancing around, wondering
if this is the right way, noticing for the first time
faces with foreheads, flowered wallpaper, tree limbs
outside the window waving in the wind —
                                          buried,
(yet recollected now, as he listens to a stranger speak),
contained since childhood with these primary things,
an elusive story he had heard —
                                      that from the bottom
of a deep well one could look up and see the stars,
even in daytime. Or that a brick chimney, if only
high enough, afforded the same sort of magical view.

This reported by a playmate, perhaps, or a cousin,
someone already old enough to read, whose authority
could not be questioned.
                         The story stayed with him
as he entered school — untested at first, half forgotten,
but a recurrent daydream, a lasting puzzlement.
Never had there been occasion to descend to the bottom
of a well, but several times, as a youth, he had crawled
inside an ash-caked furnace, in some abandoned mill
or factory, for a chance to peer up through the chimney,
hoping that somehow it might be so, that a great shaft
of darkness could transform light itself, softening
and absorbing it in some mysterious way.
                                         The stars
would be visible and gleaming at the end of that space,
as though seen through the aperture of a telescope
and yet there would be no lens, no distortion, no need
to focus. They would blaze forth with a purity
never witnessed before. But of course none of this
was true. Look up through any tall brick chimney,
all you see is a featureless patch of sky.
                                  Not so, then,
even unsound, having no basis in science or fact —
until now, years later, the myth almost forgotten,
he listens to a man speak of a mountainous country
so far above the sea, the air so pure, that in daytime
you can see the stars. "The stars?" he asks, sensing
an old thirst returning, a lost desire, even a fear —
"How could you see the stars in the daytime?"
                                          "The air
so thin, the rest of the world so far away. Stars
of the first magnitude are visible to the naked eye,
scattered across the sky like pebbles."

                              "And the sun?"
"Clear, but unapproachable — a half-remembered dream,
a shining that was rich and resplendent once, near
at hand, but now remote. No more a golden visage
but a mask of bronze."
                    He realizes that inevitably
he must find a way to visit this far place, he will
book passage on a sailing ship, after a long voyage
they will enter the harbor, he will begin to ascend
the rough-hewn steps, he will walk the cobblestones,
will enter the great palaces of perpetual dusk.
                                         There
he will encounter the serenity of the shell's interior,
the dim pearl light spreading through every corridor,
along each windowsill, across the roofs of burnt tile.
Transfixed, he will gaze far across the gaunt, gray hills,
the countryside enclosed by mountains like the shaft
of an invisible well. And in that gathering stillness
will reach out and feel a wind rising all around him,
an unseen curvature, a constantly unfolding whorl
of currents drawn up through the chalice of space.

Everything will be lifted, imperceptibly carried along,
yet nothing will be changed except the light's essence.
Even now, at noon, in a place he seems to recognize,
to know already, in his dreams, his longing — there,
on the horizon, the sun's disc hangs distant and pale,
without blemish, no longer tentacled with fire; above
the mountain peaks, at the farthest edges of the earth,
the features of the moon have all but ebbed away.

With each step he takes, there is a new awareness —
barely discernible at first, but gradually accepted,

believed in at last — everywhere he passes through
movement itself, a shifting twilight, an overflowing
of light and dark — something that was always present
at dusk or daybreak, even in childhood, but takes time
to understand, to adjust to, like the first remembrance
of water, its clear, cold taste — the light of the stars
eddying around him, softly altering, in all directions,
everything he looks upon. Stars in daylight, casting
a myriad of shadows on that rocky, wind-struck world.

Truth to Tell

> *Vous n'êtes que les masques sur des faces masquées.*
> — Apollinaire

Start, then, with a sense of beginning, of sleep
entered like a metal door backstage — the weight
of heavy, plush curtains lifted and folded, hanging
motionless, while the catwalk sways, and winches
and pulleys creak. It is no longer rest one seeks,
but mastery — the knowledge of ways to choose
among strands of rope rising into the dark, boxes
of switches, levers to be thrown, dials gleaming.

The action comes closer now — the murmur of voices
tinged with laughter, issuing from the cavernous space
beyond the footlights. And sporadic applause, followed
by music. But though this mattered once, though dreams
well up in this way, too, with easy, delicious abandon,
and sleep has its own texture — the painted faces seem
familiar, even your father is here, looking the way
he always did — still, this is only rehearsal. Truth to tell,

there is no one out there except the director, sitting
with his clipboard, thirty seats back. In the wings,
the pianist goes over the same simple tune. Yes,
there are spotlights, from a place you cannot see,
and scenery rises and falls, and darkened figures
glide across the stage during blackout, rearranging
the furniture — all this is happening, yet it goes on
whether you reach out, or whether you simply watch.
But they have lost the script, or dropped the only copy.

Its pages flutter across the stage, lifted by a cold wind
blowing from the air shaft, swirling up from the alley
and the blank walls beyond. Fluorescent lights flicker
in the wardrobe room. In the corridor, the red EXIT sign
glimmers. All of this is waiting. You must write it now,
you must make it happen. There are only a few days left
until opening night. Come, then. Rest, slumber, dream,

take my hand, we will visit the forgotten dressing rooms
under the stage, where the old tragedians scrawled verses
on the bare planks. We will go up into the attic, above
the chandeliers and the catwalks, where silence settles
like a fine dust on the broken props, on the trunks filled
with ruined costumes. Will they arrive in time, these truths
to tell, this chorus of voices? I am convinced of it.
Let us each take a part, let us begin the first reading.

Nether Moon

Now comes the moon
that rises in harsh times
of war, or discontent,
or desolation of the people.
Now, under rotting wood,
the soft tick of millipede
and pill-bug at their work,
the gnawing, the taking away
of all that mattered once.

The nether moon studies
such transformations,
watches redwoods topple,
sees rock slides churn
down vast slopes, monitors
the ocean's rise and fall.
Even the ant, its shred
of dry leaf held aloft,
does not escape notice.

In rain forest, or beneath
pine-needles washed up
in shoals, in sandy places,
or where waters rush by,
creatures appear among
interstices, foraging
what has fallen. What
hawk has dropped, bear
broken, dingo abandoned.

Nether. Never quite far,
where life goes on with
clear intent, where structure
crumbles and disappears,
leaves wither and sink,
stump becomes fragments.
Under the moon's gaze,
the pieces begin to shine
with a soft, silver light.

What Is Dream?

What is dream, ultimately, but a testing
of darkness, a venture out into that world,
the bourne from which no traveler returns?
I heard two voices from the deep. The first,
"Is he betrayed, are night and permanence
unmoored, so that the shifting sense seems right,
and nothing stays?" The other quick to answer,
"Boundless this voyage, as to the farthest star
this heading, midst the stellar silence, yet
a thousand thousand times, and still he glides,
encountering nothing." "It is well. Each dream
is but a childish step, away from all
familiarity or face. The void
that will be his eternally takes on
a pleasant guise, and seems a touch away,
almost within his grasp." *And softly said,
dear heart, how like you this?* So they spoke on,
and by the dawn that broke — the even light
that came into the room — the dream dispelled,
and I was back once more amid the sound
of wakening birds and wind-beguiling trees.

Four

Sphinx

It lives on, and with each new day, asks
the old questions, of strangers passing by,
or even of itself. Often I have heard it
calling across the wastes, like a hot wind
that brings no relief, that sorts through
acres of sand, dust, shards, broken stones,
finding nothing. Out of Egypt it came,
aeons ago, to stand at the crossroads
while travelers, in the distance, approach.

Oedipus spoke with it, though that exchange
is lost, and all manner of false stories
sprang up in later years. Of all myths,
all tales, it is the most ancient and remote,
the most elemental. Each time it appears,
like some presence that casts no shadow,
it is the wayfarer whose life has changed,
not the Sphinx, which is outside history,
and uncaring, like the oldest of sibyls.

Each time you hear its muttered questions
they strike you in a different way, though
whether you go on two legs, or four,
or three, is of little consequence now.
Rather, you must continue along the path
through rocky places, over drifted sands,
past steep ascents rising to the mountains.
The Sphinx at such moments walks beside you,
neither leading nor following, asking
or answering. It has sojourned here before,
and watches to see which way you will turn.

Colossi of Memnon

Early we woke, before dawn, with torches
borne by men who knew the way, to be led
out through the peaks and valleys of tents
heavy with shadow.
                    At the river's edge
six rowers held their tapered oars aloft.
Across that darkness, then, to the far shore,
and a road, where the dust, still drugged
with dew, no longer rose to question what
we sought in that forgotten world.
                            Ahead,
emerging from a field where nothing grew,
two battered figures loomed, as if to watch
our slow approach. No other thing was there;
far to our backs, no light had yet appeared.
The torches, moved about, revealed the ruin
of what had been a place of majesty
and power — two seated kings, worn down
by wind and sand, and accidents of time.
The northern statue had become a shrine
that somehow, in its fractured state, still kept
the power of prophecy.
                          Travelers had come,
for centuries now, to wait until the light
crept down its broken face, hoping to hear
some burst of sound, some inexplicable gasp
of ancient syllables, even — they say —
a kind of music. The guides began to speak
their lines:

"O vast, O dread magnificence,
erected to inspire, but cast adrift,
abandoned in this empty realm, speak now
of vanity, ambition, and of pride — "
We turned away, embarrassed by such show,
such falsity.
              And yet the light descended,
warming the weathered stones.
                        Something within
began to gravitate, and with a surge,
forced syllables into the unmoved air —
a curse, perhaps, for all that had transpired
to bring us to this place?
                  We stood amazed.
Is witnessing a power that outlasts kings?
I saw, it croaked, and then a torrent came:
I saw it happen, all — the trenches swift
with blood and gore, the standards thrust aloft,
the triumph through the streets, the shouts and cries,
the lifted crown!
                  But was it sense we heard,
or was that groaning but a screech of stone
digressed, unsettled by the sun's assault?
Nothing remains mysterious for long.
All was revealed by daylight, and by swirls
of dust and heat that amplified the noise
of men — confusion, commerce, common toil.
Let us go back.
              What did we hear? Some boy,
perhaps, squeezed up between the porous stones,
making crude noises?
                  "One would compare
the sound most nearly to the broken chord

of harp or lute," one ancient wrote. "A blow,"
another said, "upon an instrument
of copper."
                Even now, in places where
the faithful come, beneath revolving fans,
where water, drifting across tranquil pools,
keeps whispering — at intervals, amid
the laughter, and the subtle ebb and flow
of pleasant talk — a momentary hush
comes over everything.
                        Far off, almost
too faint to hear, some dread immensity
still seeks to find its way across the sands.

Senmurv

> *The method employed was an interesting one: a huge silver dish was heated till it was red hot, after which "the strongest vinegar" was poured over it. The Patriarch was obliged to stare directly into it for a long time, thereby utterly destroying his sight.*
> — John Julius Norwich,
>   *Byzantium: The Early Centuries*

He was christened Justinian — the second so called,
a man as evil as his namesake was honorable.
Behind his back they called him *Rhinotmetus*,
or "Cut-Nose." True, he suffered during the revolt,
but he was not put to death.
                              Fourteen years later,
his exile ended and the usurpers beheaded,
those plotters who had maimed him now blinded
and exiled in turn, he sought out more victims,
and the Terror continued.
                         As it would be written
by Paul the Deacon, "as often as he wiped away
drops of rheum from his nostrils, almost as often
did he order another of those who had opposed him
to be slain."
             Years later, one of the survivors told
of the cruelty. "We were taken to the city in chains.
When we were led before him, he sat on a throne
of gold and emeralds. He wore a diadem of gold
encrusted with pearls, fashioned by the Empress
with her own hands. All who had come with me
from Ravenna he sentenced to immediate death.
They were dragged from the hall.

                        Two eunuchs
removed my fetters, and bade me take refreshment
from a long table, where fresh figs, pomegranates,
and smoked ortolans were laid on great silver dishes.
The platters were beautifully wrought, fashioned
in some faraway place, one with a winged griffin,
others with a phoenix, an eagle, a peacock,
a caparisoned horse.
                I had eaten nothing for days.
On his throne, the Emperor dabbed at the place
where his nose had been.
                        'He welcomes Felix,
Holy Patriarch of Ravenna,' a Chamberlain said
in perfect Latin, 'and bids His Reverence partake
of the bounty offered here.' I reached for grapes.
The Emperor clapped his hands.
                        A eunuch
thrust me aside, scattered the grapes, and held
the heavy platter aloft for all to see. It bore
a fantastic silver image, a creature half bird,
half dog. 'Senmurv!' he cried out. 'Senmurv!'
echoed the courtiers, 'Senmurv!' they called,
again and again, as I was led from the chamber,
amid great laughter.
                        They sewed my eyelids back
with strands of silk. The creature on the plate
was the last thing I saw in this life. When the liquid
burned away, the heathen image opened like a star
inside my head."
                        Two years later, Justinian II
was beheaded by still more usurpers. Assassins
sent by the new Emperor pursued his grandson,
Tiberius, who was six years old, the last survivor
of the Heraclian line.

          The Old Empress hurried him
into the Church of the Virgin at Blachernae,
claiming sanctuary, pleading with the two men.
John Strouthos, called "the Sparrow," advanced
on the terrified child, who with one hand clung
to the altar and with the other clutched a piece
of the True Cross.
          Strouthos wrenched the relic
from his grasp, reverently laid it upon the altar,
took the boy outside, stripped him of his clothes,
and "slaughtered him like a sheep."
          "Senmurv,"
Felix remembered, years later, while speaking
with a chronicler from Venice, who had come
to pay his respects. "Senmurv. It is a word
that comes to me occasionally, as I sit
day after day in this shadowless room, listening
to one of the novices read aloud.
          Some mornings,
after mass, a brother will take me for a walk
through the city, and along the old fortifications,
and out into the fields.
          He might guide me to a wall
of holy images — Apollinare in Classe, perhaps,
or San Vitale. The Tomb of Galla Placidia
is my favorite. I reach as high as I can, taking in
the texture, running my fingertips over the tiles."

Kloster Wienhausen

southeast of Celle, in Lower Saxony

Down a single long passageway with many wooden doors,
doors that are closed now, that once opened into rooms painted
with Biblical scenes, rooms with windows of stained glass —

there is nothing here at all except the darkness, the light
that comes from either end of the corridor, and these fifty chests,
all made of wood, with their great hinged lids, their iron locks.

For this is the passageway of chests, enormous square boxes
made of sycamore and white oak, that have been waiting here
for half a millennium. Here, where everything is made of wood

and nothing moves, all is silence. This is the Kloster Wienhausen,
established in the thirteenth century by the Cistercian Order,
where the unwed daughters of the nobility were put away for life —

the reasons now being long forgotten, unremembered, lacking
records of any sort, except these gaunt wooden chests. Whatever
name you might choose is inadequate — cupboard, casket, safe —

since they are all that remains. The tour guide explains they held
the dowry of each young woman who was consigned to this life —
one became a bride of Christ, during the process of initiation —

while the guidebook says they contained "personal effects."
Linen, and cloth for habits, and perhaps traces of silk. Not
combs, not jewelry. These are enormous rough chests, made

at the behest of some duke or landgrave. One can imagine
carpenter and apprentice, in a courtyard, hammering and sawing,
assembling the huge planks, fitting them together with mortise

and tenon. Each stands beside the door of what were simply
dormitory rooms. The printing of books had not yet been invented,
the New World had not been imagined. You came here for life.

All that was half a millennium ago. The chests are empty now.
They are older than Leonardo and Michelangelo, older than America.
One tries to imagine something that happened to them, other than

this silence, but it cannot be done. Not some young gallant,
saying farewell to his beloved, knowing she is convent bound,
seeing the chest ready for the journey, and, to lessen her burden,

climbing inside, closing the lid, pretending he will always be there.
Not some poor soldier fleeing the Protestant army, hidden away
by the nuns, crouched in one of these enormous chests. All of that

is romanticism, fabrication, embroidery. None of that now.
The boards of the pine floor creak as you walk down the row.
Each of these chests is without decoration, each slightly different,

each still waiting.

Menuki

A found poem consisting of captions describing specific menuki displayed in the Asian Wing of the Dayton Art Institute. Menuki, sometimes called sword fittings, are pairs of tiny sculptures traditionally secured to the hilt of a samurai sword in order to improve the grip. Hammered from sheets of copper or alloys of silver and gold, they are held in position on either side of the hilt by a silk braid.

Each in the form of a cluster of branches and a flowering plum
Each in the form of celestial dragons
Each in the form of a cluster of flowers wrapped around a rolled mat
Each in the form of a crane with spread wings
    nestled amidst the upper branches
        of an ornamental spreading pine

One in the form of a prancing stag
    the other in the form of a stag nuzzling a recumbent doe
One in the form of a cluster of grasses with a crescent moon
    the other of grasses with the new moon
Each in the form of Mount Fuji

One in the form of a court noble in military dress
    the other in the form of a sage holding a book
Each in the form of a woven basket filled with sprays of flowers
Each in the form of a cluster of eggplants
One in the form of a crane taking flight
    the other in the form of a heron

Each in the form of a cluster of peacocks
Each in the form of a crawfish and waterweeds
Each in the form of crickets and wildflowers
Each in the form of two galloping horses

One in the form of a nightingale in flight
        the other in the form of the moon
Each in the form of a horse cleaning itself
        beside a shallow stream

One in the form of a stalking tiger
        the other in the form of a seated tiger
Each in the form of a fisherman walking
        with a large wicker basket

Each in the form of a samurai astride a galloping horse
Each in the form of three Chinese sages playing *go*
Each in the form of a gold pheasant
        backed by a cluster of *kiku*, millet,
                wildflowers, and grasses

Each in the form of a fisherman poling a boat

War

In Goya's "Disasters of War," print
after print of huddled women, already
raped, beaten, defeated, struggling
to bring a cup of water to another —

hillsides draped with bodies of the dead,
a priest tied to a stake, darkness,
stones, illumination within that world
always stark, unforgiving, wild —

yet in scene after scene the backgrounds
begin to dominate, the fierce stippling
and cross-hatching that never seems
to repeat itself, and is always different

from one print to the next — the void,
the emptiness, that we see swirling
and drifting about in the images
of Dürer, Rembrandt, Van Gogh —

quantum vacuum, beyond the limits
of the imagination, but shown, particles
popping into existence, screaming
on a frequency we cannot pick up —

and yet perfectly composed, balanced,
this darkness, this light that Goya bestows
on these huddled figures, these creatures
with bat wings, poring over their ledgers.

At the Art Institute

Once when I was in Chicago
up on the second floor
of the Art Institute, looking
at all the Impressionists
and the post-Impressionists
and the Fauves and the Cubists,
there was this man pushing
his mother in a wheel-chair.

Now and then, under his breath,
he called her "Mother."
He pushed her right up
to every painting in the room,
and read from the placard
as though announcing
departures and arrivals
in some busy air terminal —
the title of this particular work,
the years during which
the artist lived, the painting's
place in the history of art,
the medium, and the year
of acquisition.
                    Slowly, patiently,
from one painting to the next,
he guided the creaking machine,
placing her squarely in front
of each canvas, then beginning
to read aloud in a nasal whine.
Other patrons in the room
stared and shook their heads.

Within those huge frames
the world of La Belle Époque
blazed with sudden color
and patches of dappled light,
while the names themselves
came back like a lost litany —
Renoir and Manet, Pissarro,
Sisley, Monet, and Degas —
all mispronounced, all
strangely transformed
by his harsh calling out.

The woman in the wheel-chair
ignored the others in the room.
Her eyes were hooded, her body
gnarled and shrunken —
                              she gripped
the tubular metal arm-rests
and peered up at the paintings
while her son recited the names
and reeled off the explanations.

So on they labored, backwards
through the nineteenth century,
finally entering the precincts
of the salon painters, the creators
of *les grandes machines,* of early
Puvis de Chavannes and late
Bougereau — vast historical
and mythological compositions
that filled entire walls — the light
in those frames becoming more dim
and muddy with each step he took,
each turn of the creaking wheels

on the contraption in which
he pushed her along —
                              he continuing
to bark out the words, but neither
of them really seeing the paintings
any longer, both of them caught up
in something they insisted on
accomplishing, some witnessing
that overwhelmed them now,
some courage or indomitability
or reprise of moment long ago —

and in this manner they passed
from view, down the hallways
and through the long corridors,
until I could hear them no more.

Five

Slab Wood

One

I pulled over right where he wanted out — south of the lock
and the dam, this side of the sawmill, between the river
and the blacktop road. He'd been away for a long time,
and he wanted to walk into town on his own. We talked
for a while, looking out at the yard, at the mounds of sawdust,
logs chained to flatbeds, raw boards stacked in layers —
the best of the oak and maple going for veneer, he explained,
the rest of it cut up into fence posts, railroad ties, pallets.
What's left is slab wood, banded with thin steel, forked off
in bundles ten feet long, too heavy for one man to lift,
not much good for anything except firewood. On each slab
the sawn ends were still fresh and clean, the bark side gray,
the cut side light, almost yellow. Last year's piles of slab —
weather-beaten, dark as lumps of coal — glistened with damp.

Two

He had mentioned a place down-river. Back in the Twenties
they had thirty men on the payroll, sawing out button blanks.
After he got out, I turned the car around. At the cut-off,
field corn stood chaff-pale, the shadows between the rows
a chalky brown. Up close, the fence line showed foxtail
tufted and drooping, clusters of sumac turning to scarlet.
Willows followed the stream bed, climbing toward bluffs
of sandstone, rough knobs thrusting up from the flood plain.
Beyond these outcroppings, the river came into view — broad
and smooth, with layers of mist gathering. High above,

near the ridge, oaks covered the down slopes, their leaves
gone brown and stiff. Thickets of poplar held up branches
like strands of twisted wire. And through it all, scattered
at random in the gray light, the lantern gleam of sugar maples.

Three

Down again, the way he told me, past the DEAD END sign,
past the dock tethered to iron poles, the skiffs dragged out
and set on blocks, the shacks with their tanks of bottled gas,
windows covered with particle board and polyurethane.
I could hear talk-show laughter. No one came to look out.
I parked at the end, and followed the path to the point —
nothing but broken shell underfoot, slivers and parings,
stands of water hemlock, cat-tail. Rain blurred the far side
of the river. Poplars came up through the foundation stones.
Two original piers, laid without mortar, were still standing.
In the saw-grass, just as he had said, I found thousands
of mussel shells, whole and in pieces, their outsides blistered
with scale and grit, each one shot-gunned — sawed out
with three or four holes the size of nickels or quarters.

Four

"Plastic," he had said, just before he got out of the car.
He reached to touch the radio's knobs. "About twenty-six
or seven, plastic buttons came in, and shell fishing just went
straight to hell. Nobody wanted buttons made from shells.
The factory shut down, along about twenty-nine or thirty."
He had gone away, and come back, many times. A Seabee
during the war, stationed in the Marianas. "But even now,"
he said, "a man can get a skiff, a good rake, and a boy

to handle the oars, and if he knows what he's doing, he can
fill up that boat in five minutes. It's like 'sang," he added,
"people will pay hard cash for shell, if you know where
to take it. The Japanese crush up tons of mussel shell,
to seed artificial pearls. There's freshwater pearls, too.
A big mussel can grow a pearl as good as any oyster."

Five

He began to shiver. I offered to take him on into town,
stop at the café, have a cup of coffee, maybe a hamburger —
my treat. He said he'd been standing half the morning
west of Dubuque, couldn't get a ride, those big semis kept
blowing right on by. He lit a last cigarette, then started
to cough, bent over, crumpling the empty pack in his hand.
"Sorry," he said, straightening up. "Didn't get much to eat
these last few days." I held out three dollars. He took them.
"People in the town," he said, reaching for the door handle,
"they don't remember me. They won't like my coming back.
A man has to be careful. They don't believe there's pearls
out there in those bends, as big as a cat's eye. You go on
to that place I told you about. I thank you for your kindness."
He slipped out through the stacks of slab wood and was gone.

Up in Michigan

> *How do we know when it's God?*
> — Dan Wakefield

In what way do we encounter the holy?
How do we know it to be genuine?
A friend told me once of being on top
of another man's wife, and noticing
something cold and sharp set against
the bridge of his nose. Even in the dark
he knew it had the heft of a shotgun.
"Double-barreled, twelve-gauge,"
someone said. Two hammers clicked.
Awaken now, the dream recedes.

A light switched on. When his pupils
adjusted, he could look all the way up
both barrels, as though peering into
two long, metallic tunnels, and see
far away, like stars, the paper wadding
of each shell, bunched up, crimped,
ready to enter his skull. Louder now,
the husband, verging on incoherence,
asking him, over and over again, why?
From a great distance, someone beckons.

I think it would be like that. It could be
no other way. You would know this was
the thing itself. That you were suddenly
in the presence of the ultimate. My friend
explained that he tried to focus on the voice

and its terrible immediacy, but by the smell,
he realized his sphincters had given way,
his bladder had emptied, he had lost control
of everything except this great need to listen.
Come near, I have something to tell you.

Strangely, at that moment, he remembered
his father, dead on the gurney, wrapped in
loose green scrubs, only his face showing,
the vitality gone, the retreat into nothingness
begun — but supremely peaceful, as though
something he had encountered, sacred
and unnamable, all of his life, had finally
revealed itself. As though he had heard
the voice, and at last come face to face.
All that was but prelude to this moment.

And the solution? With no way out,
both barrels pressed between his eyes,
his loins soured by his own excrement,
"somehow I managed to talk to him,"
he told me, years later. "I kept on talking,
until he put it down. He had tossed her
across the room. She got up, made coffee.
I managed to get my clothes on. I left.
I never saw either one of them again."
Flat stones skipping across the water.

But he had gone back, once, to the house,
a cabin on a steep bluff, on the west edge
of Torch Lake. It was abandoned, slipped
from its moorings, tilted toward the water.
"There was nothing left. Biker magazines.

Coffeepot. Porcupines find a way to get in.
They need salt, they gnaw anything touched
by humans. Broom handles, wooden spoons,
clothes pins. Chewed down, eaten away."
The widening circles merge, then disappear.

Maysville, Simon Kenton Bridge, Dusk

*The text [of the Petelia Tablet] breaks off at this point.
The scattered words that remain make no consecutive
sense. Of the last line, written from bottom to top of the
right edge of the tablet, the two last words only are
legible, 'darkness enfolding' (σκότος ἀμφτκαλυψας).*
    — Jane Harrison, *Prolegomena*
     to the Study of Greek Religion

  One

It is only by crossing over this shadowy boundary,
  over this ribbon flowing incessantly vast and smooth,
far below the suspended roadway — only by this passage
  from the lights of one shore, toward the center,

into reflections from the opposite side, where air rushes
  cool and damp through the car's open windows —
only by traveling at this hour, with no purpose at all,
  do I come to an ineluctable world. . . . One spoken aloud

on front porches, in summer evenings, in stories that accompany
  rituals of rock salt and cracked ice, the metal handle
churning the cream in its wooden pail — stories that sort out
  which great-aunt was the circuit rider, which grandfather

brought back the Springfield rifle still hanging over the fireplace,
  bayonet rusted, firing mechanism frozen — language
of early twilight, of Decoration Day and the Fourth of July,
  of the voices of womenfolk soft as moths hovering

above the window boxes, of men and boys out waving sparklers. . . .
    Or the cries of young cousins mingled with the muttering
of grandmothers, with the twinge of the cast-iron gate, the calling
    of those who go on ahead, with baskets, clippers, bunches

of peonies carried in gallon cans, the old ones showing the way
    to the right path, the cedar tree, and the exact stones. . . .
Only in this way do I begin to know, to recognize what waits
    to be rediscovered, so that it can be passed on,

and never quite forgotten, even after many years, or in places
    cold and far from home. . . . Especially do I remember nights
in a coastal city, in a maze of courtyards and quadrangles,
    when those voices seemed hushed, or long unbidden,

when claiming a quiet place in which to study after dinner
    was as difficult as studying itself. Inevitably each of us
staked out a seat in the main reading room, or a carrel
    somewhere up in the stacks, or a red leather chair

in a lounge near the special collections. I remember finding,
    in the college basement, an unlocked door, which let me in
to a janitor's storeroom, and there, among cartons of toilet paper,
    and the smells of disinfectant and sweeper's dust,

as though deep in the hold of some phantom merchant ship,
    I labored over the Tragedies and the Dark Comedies,
And came there one evening, my satchel bulging with books
    and notes for term papers, and found the new padlock.

Two

It was days of wandering, then, from one building to the next,
    before an upperclassman noticed, and showed me
a secret place to study — led me along sidewalks piled with snow
    and up to the library's second floor, then farther on,

through paneled hallways, all the way back to a corridor
    with a door left unexpectedly unlatched — key lost
permanently, curator with a soft spot for undergraduates? —
    which admitted us into a room of bolted metal shelves

filled with journals, and a single desk: The Numismatic Library.
    There I spent much of my first two or three years
cramming until closing time, occasionally out of boredom
    wandering those metal stacks and taking down at random

periodicals describing the stone currency of the Yaps, cowries
    traded in Micronesia, the later designs of Pisanello,
cast for the Sforzas. Gazing at those black-and-white plates,
    those strangely sketchy drawings — heads, torsos, faces,

inscriptions — I saw everything becoming smoother and fainter,
    the farther back one looked in time. Thus one approached
a boundary, an invisible line, a moment of crossing over . . .
    And I would see it again, years later, nearing the Ohio River.

A tobacco barn, stained black, standing out starkly against
    the frost-sharpened landscape, in the sun's decline.
I knew that if I were to approach it on foot, up the path,
    with stalks crunching beneath my feet, high grass

grown brittle in late autumn, I would begin to see through
        the slats, smell the creosote, find the door held shut
with a piece of baling wire, but balanced, ready to swing open,
        and everything would be revealed — racks of leaf hanging

golden and hushed in that stillness, like drawings of old coins,
        profiles of the illustrious rubbed smooth by handling,
the great leaves brought there, bound together, stiffening
        and dying, yet beginning to murmur, to whisper

and chafe against each other in the breeze. . . . To hear such calling
        is to cross over to the other side, to re-enter a world
of images worn away by time and sleep, to remember stories
        forever being told on front porches, evenings

under the trees, in the twilight. . . . And now there is no hesitation,
        I keep going, across the bridge and down the hallway,
into the shadows, where the leaves of all the old books
        come together, rising up in *a darkness enfolding.*

    Three

Listen, you have forgotten, but always there is a dispensation
        with food, and its sharing, especially with ice cream,
especially the way your grandfather made it, which is the way
        Jefferson made it, the way he learned from the French —

the way your grandfather showed your older brothers and sisters,
        and they showed you, long ago, there on the front porch,
all of them helping, everyone taking turns at the crank. Finally,
        when it is done, when the handle grows stiff, you unbolt

the gearbox, you lift out the paddles and scrape the thickened cream
        into the cylinder, you take away everything mechanical
and fit a single square of waxed paper over the opening,
        and slip the metal lid back on again, and cap it off

with a cork. Then cover it with more salt and ice, and a rug
        or a blanket, and carry it to some corner "to set,"
for an hour or two, until the guests have eaten all the fried chicken,
        the potato salad, the cole slaw and the sliced tomatoes.

And now it is time to bring out the home-made ice cream —
        here, beneath the front-porch light, while the aunts
sit in the swing, fanning themselves, and the uncles stand
        out by the street lamp, under the maples, having a smoke.

The moment comes, after you scrape away the crust of ice
        and pry off the lid, when you reveal the waxed paper
still cupped over the cylinder, and held in place by the cold —
        the moment when you tap at the membrane, the seal,

and each of the children is allowed to come close, to touch
        its coldness, knowing what waits beneath. Slowly
you peel it away, carefully, while everyone crowds around
        and peers, over your shoulder, to see what

has been waiting there, all this time, and is ready now.
        This is the grace that I mean. This is the presence
in the black-slatted barn, on the ridge overlooking the river,
        the leaves turning bronze there in the darkness. Voices

rising up as though from some deep spring of remembrance,
    with a sudden cool wind brushing against your face,
a touch you thought you would never know again,
    a glance you thought was gone forever — all of them

blurred as though pressed into wax or clay, smoothed by water
    and by time, but coming into focus for an instant,
the old ones, momentarily summoned, crossing over to you —
    the seal broken, at last — *here, high above the river.*

Six

Encounter

Those hotels always had a room perched on top
of the third floor. You reached it up a long stairway.
On each step your shoes scrunched bits of plaster
and twigs and fluff from abandoned birds' nests.

It was the laundry room. You climbed into a cupola
that looked out over iron standpipes, brick chimneys,
roofs patched with tar. The room would be filled up
with laundry equipment — galvanized wash-tubs,

wringers, wooden drying racks folded or broken
and stacked in corners. The walls would be stucco,
the white-wash flaking off. The windows streaked,
their missing panes taped with squares of cardboard.

From there you could look out over the whole town —
the flat roofs, the brick alleys, the grassy path
where the Pennsy tracks used to be, the parking lots
put in when the old lodge buildings came down,

and beyond all that, the water tower sticking up
above the trees. Sometimes in that same room
you'd run across an exhaust fan with a flared bell,
like an air vent on the deck of an ocean liner.

Made out of sheet metal, its motor gone, turned
on one side — the curved, dust-shrouded blades
beginning to stir in response to the difference
in air pressure caused by the door you left open

at the foot of the stairs. On the bare wood floor,
amid the jumble of buckets and stiffened mops,
where the revolving blades cast their shadows,
a patch of shuttered light darkens and blurs.

Blank Paper

Those pieces of paper — not the news clippings,
the Valentine bookmarks, the stamped envelopes —
but the blank pieces, sometimes two or three sheets
of heavy bond, and not always the same size,
as though they had been cut down carefully,
or trimmed for some special purpose — those sheets
of watermarked paper I run across in used books
in the second-hand store near the bus station,
or in the old shop the rare-book dealer's widow
still keeps open, on a side street, two days a week,
though he is gone, and the rent so high these days —

All these years I have been finding such sheets
but not been able to read them, not understand
how their blankness, their peculiar emptiness,
has always been there, tucked within those pages,
balancing the weight of the words and letters,
waiting to offer a certain clarity or freedom
to any stranger who might run across them.

I have a friend who lives out west, who dates
from the days of the Santa Fe Super Chief
and Fred Harvey's restaurants, and hours spent
in dusty hotel lobbies, waiting to close a sale.
Sometimes he writes on stationery taken
from the night tables in single rooms, stacks
of paper placed there beside the Gideon Bible,
in the drawer that never contains anything else.

Mornings, he stops at the newsstand on the square,
and buys a chromolithographed postcard showing
the memorial hospital in Atchison, Kansas,
or the boyhood home of William Jennings Bryan.
It is all blank, everything he collects, and when
he writes, he really has nothing to say. Sometimes
he simply sends empty sheets, with the letterhead
showing the façade of the New Excelsior Hotel,
or all the trucks lined up in front of the creamery.

We both know this is big country, it is replete
with empty spaces. There are people, everywhere,
who take out a few pieces of paper, maybe it is
expensive paper, they have been saving it, now
they are going to sit down and write to someone,
and say things they have always wanted to say.
But it has been a long time since they have written
anything at all, and they need a pen, they get up
to go look for one, and suddenly the phone rings —
so they slip the sheets of paper inside a book.

Do I have a gift for finding such things, years
after the fact? No, my doing so is accidental,
I am a simple man, prone to the same delays
and uncertainties as everyone else. I too began
with the best of intentions. There were truths
I dreamed of writing once, that would come
from the heart, that would make a difference.
But other things came first. My own books
began to harbor odd pieces of blank paper.

Even now, up in the attic, inside old volumes
I cannot bring myself to throw away, I find
such sheets — cream-colored and deckle-edged,
made in the last century out of discarded rags
and strips of linen.
                    And I think, yes, it is better
that they remain here, slipped among these pages.
In this way they can still offer a new beginning;
they might even be put to advantage someday.
I still believe this can happen. I still imagine
such discoveries are possible — the way light
from a lone window reaches into this corner
and manages to show these forgotten shapes.

Under the Snowball Bush

Let him crawl which yet lies sleeping
Through the deep grass of the meadow!
                — Shelley

Look not under the lilacs, with their lavender blossoms, their white,
    that stand like thickets along both sides of the garden path,
        their canes so rich, so laden, you can barely pass through;

No, nor below the spring-house, where the late wisteria clings
    to the rocks in the limestone wall, where long clusters
        of blue flowers spill down and pool in the shadows;

No, nor within the shaggy tunnel of spirea bordering the side yard,
    the spangled hedge that leans heavily now, that droops
        almost to the ground, to the scattering of violets there;

Nor among bunches of peonies lining the driveway, nor the mock orange,
    nor the clematis inching up to shade the front-porch swing,
        nor the honeysuckle nodding in a breeze that promises rain,

Not even in the pale dark of the apple tree, by the summer kitchen,
    that has lost half its branches, and leans now, propped up
        with a board, its flowers chalk white against a slate sky.

Look not in any of those places, where things open at last to the wind,
    sending their sweetness to mingle with the smell of cut grass,
        with the odor of black earth spaded and turned in the garden.

Look instead along the front walk, not quite to the wrought-iron fence,
    near the row of maples, where you can see the road from town,
        and the turn-off to the river, and there you will find

The place that I mean: there, under the snowball bush, where the grass
    is adrift with falling petals, where the white tomcat —
        the long-haired stray, with one brown eye and one blue —

Sleeps in the shadows. If you waken him, he will rise stiffly
    and step through the dappled light, stretching before you
        on the flagstones, first the front legs, then the back,

But you must help him, for he cannot remember the way. Asleep now,
    is he the wind unraveling, or simply another row of whiteness
        raked by the wind? Is he rain receding, or rain approaching?

You have only to reach out and take a branch, and shake it, slowly,
    carefully, so that the blossoms loosen from their bolls,
        so that they drift down and cover him in his dreaming.

Mourning Dove Ascending

At the moment of rising, when it takes flight
through the clearing, in the false light of dawn,
the notes of its call stay with you — a sound

you have been drawn toward all of your life,
without knowing why. Something in that voice
still has the power to summon, even as it fades,

even as the creature's wings begin to make
a different kind of music — an elusive whistling
that spreads in circles and in overlapping waves.

It is a sound more rare, more hushed than song,
issuing not from the throat but the body,
the body working against time and space,

finding purchase, trusting in the outcome
of that endeavor — the whisper and whirl
of the feathers, the vanishing into the dark.

Cicadas in the Rain

Only when it began to rain could I hear it,
in late summer, after they had all risen high
in the saucer magnolia tree — a soft, slow rain
at first, while the light still held in the west.

That sound so familiar, so unhesitant, but never
during a storm, and yet with drops plashing
and pelting through the leaves, their voices
coalesced in ways I had never heard before —

some strange harmonic of summer's ending,
some last reinforcement or challenge — mounting
against the rain's insistence, trying to outdo it,
seeking a pulse within the larger immensity,

and succeeding, as though a door had opened,
and I heard pure sound issuing forth, stately
and majestic, even golden, while all around it,
darkness, rain falling, trees bent by the wind.

Snow

At every hand there are moments we
cannot quite grasp or understand. Free

to decide, to interpret, we watch rain
streaking down the window, the drain

emptying, leaves blown by a cold wind.
At least we sense a continuity in

such falling away. But not with snow.
It is forgetfulness, what does not know,

has nothing to remember in the first place.
Its purpose is to cover, to leave no trace

of anything. Whatever was there before —
the worn broom leaned against the door

and almost buried now, the pile of brick,
the bushel basket filling up with thick,

gathering whiteness, half sunk in a drift —
all these things are lost in the slow sift

of the snow's falling. Now someone asks
if you can remember — such a simple task —

the time before you were born. Of course
you cannot, nor can I. Snow is the horse

that would never dream of running away,
that plods on, pulling the empty sleigh

while the tracks behind it fill, and soon
everything is smooth again. No moon,

no stars, to guide your way. No light.
Climb up, get in. Be drawn into the night.

Acknowledgments

The author thanks the editors of the following print and online publications where these poems — sometimes in different versions or with different titles — first appeared:

One

Prophet Township	*Valparaiso Poetry Review*
Roadside Crosses	*The Formalist*
Natural Gas Boom	*Tipton Poetry Journal*
Miss Hester	*One Trick Pony*
Difficult	*Southern Hum*
Summit	*Midwest Quarterly*

Two

Fire Burning in a 55-Gallon Drum	*The Reaper*
E. Washington Street Plasma Center	*South Street Star*
In the Warehouse District	*Yarrow*
Triage	*Poetry*
In the Military Park	*Pemmican*
The Pool at Noon	*Valparaiso Poetry Review*
Plastic Sack	*Melic Review*

Three

Hidden Door	*Valparaiso Poetry Review*
Wind Egg	*Laurel Review*
Soul Sleeping	*Poetry*
Stars in Daylight	*Visions International*
Truth to Tell	*Free Lunch*
Nether Moon	*Eclectica Magazine*
What Is Dream?	*Pennsylvania Review*

Four
Sphinx   *Chronicles*
Colossi of Memnon   *Agenda*
Senmurv   *Poeziepamflet*
Kloster Wienhausen   *Archipelago*
Menuki   *Nexus*
War   *Valparaiso Poetry Review*
At the Art Institute   *The Scream Online*

Five
Slab Wood   *The Heartlands Today*
Up in Michigan   *Melic Review*
Maysville, Kenton Bridge, Dusk   *Down the River*

Six
Encounter   *American Literary Review*
Blank Paper   *Midwest Quarterly*
Under the Snowball Bush   *Fennel Stalk*
Mourning Dove Ascending   *Evansville Review*
Cicadas in the Rain   *North Dakota Quarterly*
Snow   *Poetry*

The poem "Senmurv" is based in part on three passages in John Julius Norwich's *Byzantium: the Early Centuries*, published in the U.S. in 1988 by Knopf. Lord Norwich's footnote on p. 340 serves as the poem's epigraph. Paul the Deacon's remarks on Justinian II are quoted by Norwich on p. 338. The poem's invented narrative of the blinding of Archbishop Felix in 709 was prompted by Norwich's account on p. 340. Poem lines 58-68 describing the murder of Justinian's grandson condense and paraphrase Norwich's paragraph found on pp. 344-45. These borrowings are reprinted by permission of the publisher, Alfred E. Knopf, and are gratefully acknowledged.

"Prophet Township" was selected for the print anthology, *Best of the Web 2008*, edited by Steve Almond and Nathan Leslie and published by Dzanc Books.

The front-cover photo, "Day," by *New York Times* photographer Edward Hausner, shows one of four pairs of allegorical female figures representing *Time* that originally appeared above the four entryways to New York City's Pennsylvania Station. Each figure weighed ten tons and was part of an ensemble that was fourteen feet long and eleven feet high.

The figure of "Day" held behind her head a garland of sunflowers, while "Night" grasped two poppies, flowers traditionally associated with sleep. These eight "stone maidens" were among dozens of monumental figures carved by the German-born sculptor Adolph Alexander Weinman (1870-1952).

Penn Station, designed by the architectural firm of McKim, Mead and White, was completed in 1910. It was considered an outstanding example of the Beaux-Arts style. During 1963 and 1964, the above-ground portion of the original structure was demolished. In the 1970s the continuing uproar over the demolition of such a well-known landmark became a catalyst for the architectural preservation movement in the United States.

Debris from the building's demolition was dumped in a landfill at the Meadowlands in New Jersey, where Edward Hausner took the photograph in 1968.

The author thanks the following readers for their suggestions for improving the manuscript of this book: Diane Carter, Kevin Cutrer, David Lee Garrison, Paul Hurt, Patrick Kanouse, Mark Latta, Steve Phillips, John Robertson, and Leo Yankevich.

About the Author

Jared Carter lives in Indiana. He has been a recipient of the Walt Whitman Award of the Academy of American Poets, the Poets' Prize, a fellowship from the John Simon Guggenheim Memorial Foundation, and two literary fellowships from the National Endowment for the Arts. Information concerning his previous books of poetry may be found on his web site *Jared Carter Poetry* and on his blog *Rushing the Growler*.

http://jaredcarter.com
http://www.the-growler.com